TAKING A STAND

LARRY ITLIONG
LEADS THE WAY FOR FARMWORKERS' RIGHTS

by Rose Zilka

FOCUS
READERS

www.focusreaders.com

Copyright © 2019 by Focus Readers, Lake Elmo, MN 55042. All rights reserved. No part of this book may be reproduced or utilized in any form or by any means without written permission from the publisher.

Focus Readers is distributed by North Star Editions:
sales@northstareditions.com | 888-417-0195

Produced for Focus Readers by Red Line Editorial.

Content Consultant: Todd Holmes, PhD, Historian and Academic Specialist, University of California Berkeley Bancroft Library Oral History Center

Photographs ©: Walter P. Reuther Library/Archives of Labor and Urban Affairs/Wayne State University, cover, 1, 17, 19, 30; Philip Brigandi/Stereograph Cards/Library of Congress, 4–5; Farm Security Administration/Office of War Information/Library of Congress, 6; Dorothea Lange/Farm Security Administration/Office of War Information/Library of Congress, 8–9, 14–15, 20–21, 23, 25; Dorothea Lange/Library of Congress, 11; George Birch/AP Images, 13; Harold Filan/AP Images, 26–27; Red Line Editorial, 29, 36; Marion S. Trikosko/U.S. News & World Report Magazine Photograph Collection/Library of Congress, 32–33, 39; Walter Zeboski/AP Images, 35; Richard Thornton/Shutterstock Images, 40–41, 42, 45

Library of Congress Cataloging-in-Publication Data
Library of Congress Cataloging-in-Publication Data is available on the Library of Congress website.

ISBN
978-1-64185-356-9 (hardcover)
978-1-64185-414-6 (paperback)
978-1-64185-530-3 (ebook pdf)
978-1-64185-472-6 (hosted ebook)

Printed in the United States of America
Mankato, MN
October, 2018

ABOUT THE AUTHOR

Rose Zilka is a writer and educator. In her work, she explores how communities form and the ways individuals connect to the people and places around them. She lives in Saint Paul, Minnesota.

TABLE OF CONTENTS

CHAPTER 1

STRIKE!

On September 8, 1965, hundreds of Filipino American farmworkers piled into Filipino Hall in Delano, California. Filipino Hall was a gathering space for the farmworkers. Usually, they held dances and celebrations in the hall. But tonight, they were not there to dance or celebrate. The workers had a decision to make.

Delano was one of California's numerous farm towns. The city had many large **vineyards**.

Farmworkers pick grapes on a 5,000-acre vineyard in Guasti, California, in 1923.

Farmworkers often lived in labor camps, such as this one in Sonoma, California, in 1937.

Most of the vineyards were owned by wealthy white men. These men, known as growers, hired farmworkers to help at harvest time. Many of the farmworkers were **immigrants** from the Philippines and Mexico. Because of Delano's many vineyards, the area had become home to a large immigrant population.

In Filipino Hall, Larry Itliong gave a speech to his fellow farmworkers. Itliong was a respected leader in the Filipino farmworker community. He spoke to the workers about the **discrimination** they experienced on the job. Most vineyard owners expected the immigrant farmworkers to work long, unreasonable hours. And they paid the workers barely enough money to survive. In his speech, Itliong encouraged the workers to take a stand against Delano growers.

Itliong wanted the Filipino farmworkers to go on **strike**. If the workers agreed, they would stop working until the growers agreed to pay them a fair wage. But going on strike was risky. The growers might find other people to replace the Filipino workers. If that happened, the workers could lose their jobs. However, Itliong saw striking as their only opportunity for change.

For a strike to succeed, the workers had to stand together. Itliong called for a vote, and the workers all agreed. Tomorrow, they would walk out of the vineyards and begin their strike.

CHAPTER 2

THE MANONGS

By the 1930s, thousands of young Filipino men had immigrated to the United States. The majority of these men found jobs as **migrant** farmworkers. Previously, many US growers had depended on Japanese workers to harvest their crops. But due to changing immigration laws, people from Japan were no longer able to move to the United States. Growers struggled to find enough workers at harvest time.

A Filipino farmworker cuts cauliflower near Santa Maria, California, in 1937.

To get more workers, growers told young men from the Philippines that they could find happiness and wealth in the United States. However, when the men arrived, very few were able to live the lives they had been promised.

During the 1920s and 1930s, US laws discriminated against immigrants. Filipinos were unable to own land, vote, or start businesses. Many of the men had no choice but to continue working in the fields. The law also prohibited Filipinos from marrying anyone who was not Filipino. Since immigration laws were so strict, very few Filipino women were able to move to the United States. As a result, most of the Filipino farmworkers never married.

Because few Filipino farmworkers had families of their own, the men became like brothers. Younger Filipinos referred to the first wave of

▲ Filipino farmworkers used this makeshift bathroom at a labor camp in Coachella, California.

Filipino immigrants as *manongs*. In Ilocano, a native language in the Philippines, *manong* means "older brother."

Manongs formed tight-knit communities across the West Coast. They helped one another deal with poor living conditions. Most manongs lived in labor camps provided by the growers. But the camps were never clean, and often there weren't enough beds.

The manongs' working conditions were even worse. At the time, no laws protected Filipinos' safety on the job. They worked long hours without breaks. Some workers didn't have access to water or bathrooms. If temperatures were dangerously hot, growers still expected them to work the full day. On top of poor working conditions, manongs were not paid enough to support themselves.

Although they were mistreated, manongs depended on growers to get by. Without their jobs, the workers would have no shelter or food. But their dependence on growers did not stop them from fighting back. Since the 1920s, the Filipinos had built a reputation for negotiating. They even held short strikes to win higher wages.

The workers were strategic. They specialized in harvesting the most difficult crops, such as asparagus and grapes. Growers were willing to

▲ An elderly manong picks grapes in a California vineyard in 1970.

pay the men more for harvesting these crops. For this reason, the manongs were paid more than most other farmworkers.

However, the manongs were growing older. They would not be able to keep up with their jobs for much longer. Their backs ached, and their arms were sore. But if they stopped working, they would have nowhere to live and no food to eat. In 1965, when Itliong began speaking of another strike, the men were ready.

CHAPTER 3

SEVEN FINGERS

Larry Itliong emigrated from the Philippines to the United States in 1929. He was only 15 years old at the time. Larry came from a poor family. He had never slept in a bed or lived in a house with electricity. His living conditions in the United States weren't much better. When he arrived in the country, he found work as a migrant farmworker. He traveled among states on the West Coast to harvest many types of crops.

Filipino farmworkers cut and load lettuce in Imperial Valley, California, in 1937.

No matter where Larry worked, he noticed that one thing never changed. Farmworkers faced severe discrimination on the job.

As Larry continued to work in the fields, he met leaders who wanted to make a change. These leaders were trying to improve the way growers treated farmworkers. Larry quickly joined their fight for justice. In 1930, he helped lettuce workers in Washington fight for higher wages. The workers won, and thanks to the pay increase, their lives improved significantly.

Itliong also worked in Alaska's canneries. He helped form a **union** for cannery workers. One day,

➤ THINK ABOUT IT

Many Filipino farmworkers were still teenagers when they moved to the United States. What do you think was the hardest part about leaving their homes?

Larry Itliong held several leadership positions in his years as a labor activist.

he lost three of his fingers in a cannery accident. After that, people called him "Seven Fingers."

Soon, Itliong became a leader among Filipino workers. In 1959, he was appointed a leader in the Agricultural Workers Organizing Committee (AWOC). This organization focused on fighting for the rights of Filipino workers in the United States.

Itliong was dedicated to his cause. He learned English, Spanish, Cantonese, Japanese, and several other languages. That way, he could communicate with a variety of people in the agricultural industry.

Itliong was a strong leader, but he was also mysterious. Workers spread stories of how Itliong lost his fingers. However, no one could get him to tell the real story. No one knew Itliong's secret to playing cards, either. Itliong often played cards with other union workers. When he won, he collected the workers' membership fees from their winnings. Itliong almost always won.

When Itliong came to California for the grape harvest season in 1965, he partnered with Philip Vera Cruz. Vera Cruz was also a leader in the AWOC. Like Itliong, Vera Cruz wanted to fight for Filipinos' rights. Together, Itliong and Vera Cruz

Itliong (second from right) speaks with a group of Brazilian farmworkers in the 1960s.

launched a strike that would go down in history. They had no idea how large the movement would become. But they knew that if they did not strike now, the lives of Filipino workers might never improve.

CHAPTER 4

RISKING IT ALL

With Itliong and Vera Cruz leading the way, AWOC members began striking in Coachella, California. In May 1965, they asked for higher wages from the Coachella growers. They succeeded, and the farmworkers received higher pay for the season. However, the growers could have said no. If this had happened, the striking farmworkers might have lost their jobs.

This 1935 photo shows children of farmworkers living in a labor camp in Coachella, California.

Itliong and Vera Cruz thought workers should be able to ask for higher wages without risking their jobs. The men wanted a **contract**. A contract would require the growers to provide fair wages every year.

The growers in Coachella refused to sign a contract. So the farmworkers moved on to Delano. Itliong was determined to get growers in Delano to sign a contract. He had seen successful strikes in Alaska and Washington. There, lettuce and canning workers had won contracts. They were able to lead better lives. Itliong wanted this change for the grape farmworkers as well. On September 8, he urged the farmworkers at Filipino Hall to go on strike.

The next day, approximately 1,000 Filipino farmworkers began the Delano Grape Strike. Some farmworkers stayed in the labor camps

▲ Lettuce farmworkers faced many of the same issues as grape pickers.

instead of going to work. Other workers **picketed**. They tried to convince workers who hadn't joined the strike to stop working. The picketers called these workers scabs. A scab, or strikebreaker, is someone who keeps working during a strike. Some picketers used violence to stop scabs.

Growers fought back, sending men to break up the picket lines. Picketing was dangerous, but it was the most effective way to recruit more strikers.

Growers forced out the striking farmworkers who stayed inside the labor camps. They turned off the water and made the living conditions unbearable. As a result, men flooded into Filipino Hall to find a place to sleep. The hall became the strikers' new home. Here, they shared meals, slept, and planned their next moves.

Despite all this work, the strike was failing. The growers were looking to hire other workers to replace the strikers. If this happened, the growers would no longer need Filipino workers, and the strike would be over. Itliong decided it was time to join forces with non-Filipino farmworkers.

For years, growers had used Mexican Americans and Filipino Americans against one another. When

Filipino and Mexican farmworkers worked side by side at this beet field in Monterey County, California.

Mexican workers went on strike, Filipinos went to work in their place. And when Filipinos went on strike, Mexicans took their place. If Mexican and Filipino farmworkers banded together, growers would have even fewer workers. Then, they would have to listen to the farmworkers' demands.

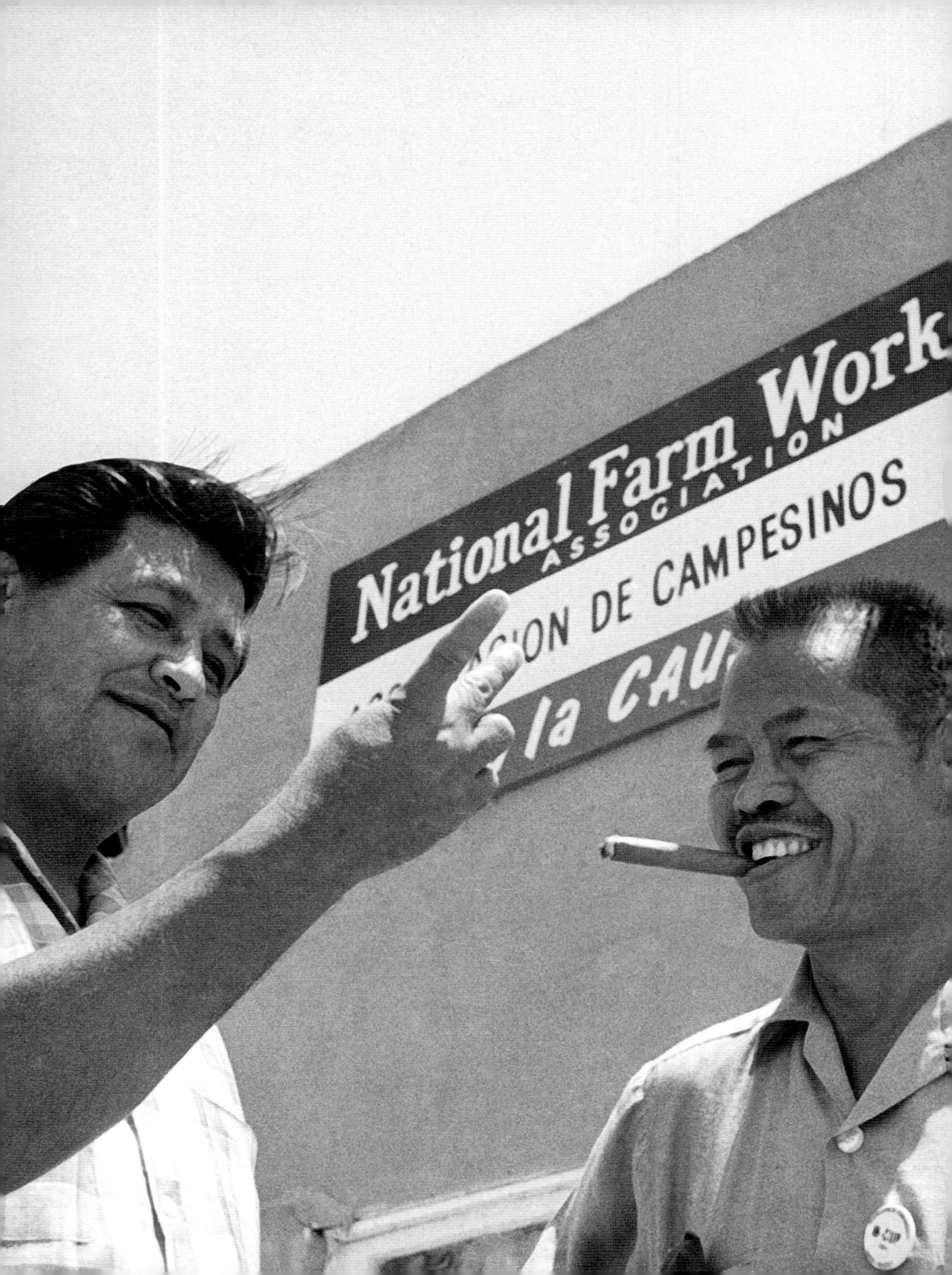

National Farm Work
ASSOCIATION
CION DE CAMPESINOS
la CAU

CHAPTER 5

JOINING HANDS

To get Mexican workers to join the strike, Itliong went to labor leader Cesar Chavez. Chavez was a successful leader among Mexican farmworkers. He was also the founder of the National Farm Workers Association (NFWA). At first, Chavez was unsure about Itliong's request. The NFWA did not have enough money or resources to support a strike. Chavez said the NFWA would be ready to join the grape strike in another two or three years.

Cesar Chavez and Larry Itliong talk in front of the NFWA headquarters in Delano, California.

But the manongs could not wait that long. The aging workers needed the protection of a contract as soon as possible.

On September 16, 1965, hundreds of Mexican farmworkers met in Delano to vote. The workers knew the chances of the strike succeeding were slim. But they still wanted to try. After the NFWA voted to join the strike, the farmworkers celebrated. They cheered, "Viva la huelga," which is Spanish for "long live the strike."

Mexican workers joined Filipinos on the picket lines. The Filipino strikers welcomed them as brothers. Filipino Hall now became home to both Mexican and Filipino farmworkers.

Chavez's vision for the strike stretched beyond the borders of Delano. He fought for the rights of all farmworkers, regardless of their background. In 1966, the AWOC and the NFWA joined to form the

United Farm Workers Union (UFW). The strike had now become a movement for all farmworkers.

To gain support, Chavez reached out to political and religious leaders across the nation. Among these leaders was US senator Robert F. Kennedy.

FARMWORKER STRIKES ACROSS THE NATION (1965–1975)

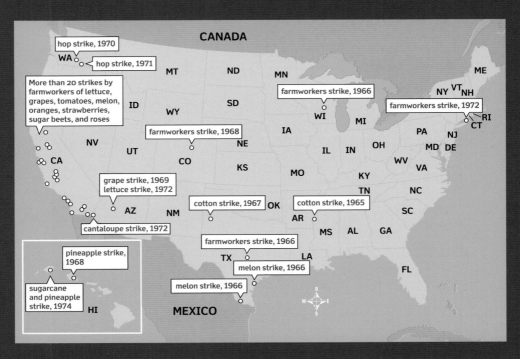

▲ Itliong stands behind Robert F. Kennedy (right) during a farmworkers' rally in Delano in 1968.

Chavez also gathered students who wanted to fight for social change. The strike was gaining more and more attention. Chavez, Itliong, Vera Cruz, and many other leaders worked tirelessly to promote their cause.

The farmworkers usually stopped striking when the growing season ended. However, now that they had the nation's attention, the UFW decided to continue. The strikers picketed outside the grape fields. Then they followed the harvested grapes up along California's border. They picketed at the docks where **longshoremen** loaded the grapes onto boats. Sometimes, fights broke out between picketers and longshoremen. But other longshoremen joined the picketers in support.

The grape strikers had the support of other labor unions. Filipino workers were experienced in forming unions. And Itliong was a well-known union leader. He called on other union leaders for support. They helped provide food, money, and other supplies to the striking workers.

So far, nothing about the strike had been easy. But as more people joined, victory seemed more and more possible.

THINK ABOUT IT ◀

Many famous leaders around the country supported the strikers. How do you think this affected the strike?

LOVING *CHEVROLET*
SILVER SPRING MD.

 **Don't Eat Grapes.**

CHAPTER 6

DON'T EAT GRAPES!

The Delano Grape Strike stretched on. Picketing at the docks had brought the strike national attention. But the success was only temporary. Soon, picketing became too violent. Fights continued to break out among strikers, scabs, and police officers. Strikers needed a different strategy.

Chavez, Itliong, and other UFW leaders came up with a two-part plan to continue the strike.

Some people supported the grape strike by putting bumper stickers on their cars.

The first part was to call for a national **boycott** of grapes. The UFW asked shoppers to stop buying grapes from Schenley Industries. Schenley was a major grower in Delano that refused to sign a contract with the UFW.

To encourage the boycott, the UFW created a symbol of an Aztec eagle. Growers that had a contract with the UFW would place the symbol on their products. If a package didn't have the symbol, shoppers knew not to buy it. Strikers also picketed outside stores that sold Schenley grapes. They held up signs that read, "Don't Eat Grapes!"

Part two of the plan was to organize a march. In March 1966, the UFW and its supporters planned to walk 340 miles (550 km) from Delano to Sacramento. During the march, Schenley Industries called UFW leaders. The grower finally agreed to sign a contract with the farmworkers.

▲ Grape strikers march to Sacramento, California, in 1966.

National attention from the march had put pressure on the growers. Plus, the boycott was costing them business. Schenley knew it was time to give up.

With sore feet and sun-beaten faces, thousands of marchers arrived in Sacramento. The marchers shouted in happiness on the steps of the state capitol. After months of protesting, they had won their first contract. It would be the first of many contracts for the UFW.

The UFW's contracts helped grape workers receive fair wages and better treatment. However, the contracts had negative effects, too. Many Filipino workers depended on labor camps for housing. But after signing the contracts, the growers decided to close the labor camps.

GRAPE STRIKE MARCH (1966)

In addition, some Filipinos didn't receive higher wages after signing the contract. The UFW made sure all farmworkers were paid fairly. However, Filipino workers were already being paid more than other farmworkers. This was because they specialized in difficult jobs. Itliong was glad the farmworkers had won a contract. But he also knew it had come as a sacrifice to Filipino workers.

The manongs had risked everything to start the strike. But because of the **publicity** Chavez and other Mexican leaders had received, Filipino workers were largely forgotten.

THINK ABOUT IT ◄

The strike helped many farmworkers, but it also hurt Filipinos. If Filipino farmworkers had known this would happen, do you think they would have agreed to strike? Why or why not?

CESAR CHAVEZ

Cesar Chavez became the face of the Delano Grape Strike. Chavez was quiet by nature and struggled with public speaking. However, his ideas inspired many. Chavez read books on St. Francis of Assisi and Mahatma Gandhi for inspiration. Like these leaders, Chavez believed nonviolence was the only way to make real change.

Farmworker strikes had a history of turning violent. Growers and strikers would fight one another on the picket lines. Growers would even throw explosives into the labor camps. But Chavez had a different vision. "Violence just hurts those who are already hurt," Chavez explained. "We can turn the world if we can do it nonviolently."

In 1968, many strikers felt discouraged. They feared the strike would never end. As a symbol of protest, Chavez fasted and drank nothing but water for 25 days. Chavez's body became weak

Chavez speaks with an interviewer in 1979.

from hunger, but he didn't give up. Soon, his fast gained national attention. More and more people became aware of the strike.

After the fast, Chavez was too weak to speak. He had someone read these words for him: "I am convinced that the truest act of courage, the strongest act of humanity, is to sacrifice ourselves for others in a totally nonviolent struggle for justice."

Evelina Alarcon. "Cesar Chavez: A Legacy for Peace, Justice and Non-violence." *People's World*. People's World, 27 Mar. 2003. Web. 27 Aug. 2018.

CHAPTER 7

LEGACY

The grape workers' strike did not end with the Delano contract. The UFW would not stop striking until every grape grower in the United States agreed to a contract. The strike lasted from 1965 to 1970, making it one of the longest strikes in the nation's history.

Although the strike had its downsides, the manongs did have one dream fulfilled. In 1974, the UFW funded Agbayani Village in Delano.

In 2016, UFW members marched in Delano to support overtime pay for farmworkers.

▲ In 2014, Dolores Huerta spoke at the 40th anniversary of Agbayani Village. She had helped lead the grape strike.

Agbayani was a **retirement** home for aging manongs who were no longer able to work. The manongs finally had a clean home with warm food and their own beds. The home allowed retired manongs to continue living together as brothers.

The Delano Grape Strike became a historic example of the power of labor unions. The strike encouraged immigrant workers to continue fighting discrimination. Farmworkers around the nation followed in the grape workers' footsteps. They formed their own unions and fought for better working conditions. Both Itliong and Chavez went on to lead further union efforts among farmworkers.

Today, most people remember the Delano Grape Strike as a Mexican movement. Very few are aware of the role Filipino farmworkers played in the strike. In recent years, the city of Delano has made efforts to recognize both Larry Itliong and Philip Vera Cruz. In 2016, Alvarado Middle School in Union City was renamed Itliong-Vera Cruz Middle School. And in 2013, California passed a law requiring public schools to teach the history of Filipino Americans' involvement in the strike. The state also made October 25 Larry Itliong Day. This holiday honors Itliong's fight for farmworkers' rights.

FRED ABAD

In 1929, 17-year-old Fred Abad moved from the Philippines to the United States. Leaving his home country wasn't easy. When Fred was older, he wrote about the day he left. "When the truck started to move, I looked through the window and saw my auntie and the girls with tears in their eyes. They cried. I hollered to them that I'd come back. I never went back."

In the United States, Abad spent his days in the fields. Later, Abad looked back fondly on his years as a farmworker. The other farmworkers became his family. And not all growers treated workers poorly. "Some of the other boys were mistreated," Abad recalled. "I was not mistreated. In fact, the growers were good to me."

Abad was one of the last residents of Agbayani Village. Many students visited him to learn about the Delano Grape Strike. The retired manong

▲ Today, the UFW has offices at Agbayani Village.

appreciated these visits. Students often brought him pictures and cards, which he hung on the wall. The students also enjoyed their visits. Abad taught them about the role Filipino Americans played in changing history.

Fred Abad. "Letter to Tom Dalzell from Fred Abad." *Farmworker Movement Documentation Project.* UC San Diego Library, 21 Jan. 1982. Web. 27 Aug. 2018.

FOCUS ON
LARRY ITLIONG

Write your answers on a separate piece of paper.

1. Write a paragraph summarizing the main ideas of Chapter 2.

2. Both Filipino and Mexican workers played important roles in fighting for farmworkers' rights. Why do you think Mexican farmworkers received more recognition?

3. Which organization did Larry Itliong help lead with Philip Vera Cruz?

   A. Agricultural Workers Organizing Committee
   B. National Farm Workers Association
   C. United Farm Workers Union

4. Which action had the greatest impact on the Delano Grape Strike?

   A. Larry Itliong convinced Mexican workers to join the strike.
   B. The UFW raised enough funds to build Agbayani Village.
   C. The AWOC convinced the Coachella growers to raise workers' wages.

Answer key on page 48.

GLOSSARY

boycott
A protest in which people refuse to buy certain goods or services.

contract
An agreement to pay someone a certain amount of money.

discrimination
Unfair treatment of others based on who they are or how they look.

immigrants
People who move to a new country.

longshoremen
People who load and unload ships in a port.

migrant
Moving from place to place to do seasonal work.

picketed
Protested by marching outside with signs.

publicity
Attention from the media.

retirement
Designed for people who are no longer working.

strike
When people stop working as a way to demand better working conditions or better pay.

union
An organization that protects the rights of workers.

vineyards
Areas of land where farmers grow grapes.

TO LEARN MORE

BOOKS

Braun, Eric. *Taking Action for Civil and Political Rights*. Minneapolis: Lerner Publications, 2017.

Brimner, Larry Dane. *Strike! The Farm Workers' Fight for Their Rights*. Honesdale, PA: Calkins Creek Books, 2014.

Gay, Kathlyn. *César Chávez: Fighting for Migrant Farmworkers*. New York: Enslow Publishing, 2018.

NOTE TO EDUCATORS

Visit **www.focusreaders.com** to find lesson plans, activities, links, and other resources related to this title.

INDEX

Answer Key: **1.** Answers will vary; **2.** Answers will vary; **3.** A; **4.** A